Computer Mouse

Robin Koontz

rourkeeducationalmedia.com

*Scan for Related Titles
and Teacher Resources*

Teaching Focus:

Vocabulary: Multiple Meanings- The word mouse and chip have multiple meanings. Can you tell how to use the words in different ways? Can you use each word in a sentence?

Before Reading:

Building Academic Vocabulary and Background Knowledge

Before reading a book, it is important to set the stage for your child or student by using pre-reading strategies. This will help them develop their vocabulary, increase their reading comprehension, and make connections across the curriculum.

1. *Read the title and look at the cover. Let's make predictions about what this book will be about.*
2. *Take a picture walk by talking about the pictures/photographs in the book. Implant the vocabulary as you take the picture walk. Be sure to talk about the text features such as headings, the Table of Contents, glossary, bolded words, captions, charts/diagrams, or index.*
3. *Have students read the first page of text with you then have students read the remaining text.*
4. *Strategy Talk – use to assist students while reading.*
    - *Get your mouth ready*
    - *Look at the picture*
    - *Think…does it make sense*
    - *Think…does it look right*
    - *Think…does it sound right*
    - *Chunk it – by looking for a part you know*
5. *Read it again.*
6. *After reading the book complete the activities below.*

Content Area Vocabulary
Use glossary words in a sentence.

computer chip
cursor
sensors
signals
switches
trackball

After Reading:

Comprehension and Extension Activity

After reading the book, work on the following questions with your child or students in order to check their level of reading comprehension and content mastery.

1. *What is a trackball? (Summarize)*
2. *How are the mouse and cursor connected? (Asking questions)*
3. *Do you use a mouse with your computer? What does it look like? (Text to self connection)*
4. *How did the mouse get its name? (Summarize)*

Extension Activity

Take a look at your computer mouse. What does it look like? Is it wired or wireless? Does it have buttons? Does it have a ball? What does it look like underneath? What happens when you click the right side button? And the left side button? Does the mouse work on a flat surface? On a rough surface? On your hand? On a mouse pad? Which surface does it work best on? Continue to experiment with your mouse and record your observations.

Table of Contents

What Is a Computer Mouse?

What kind of mouse has no ears, nose, or feet? A computer mouse!

It got its name because it looks sort of like a mouse.

The first computer mouse was a wood box with wheels and buttons.

A mouse and a computer work together.

It is like a very smart pointing stick.

Mouse Guts

There are many parts inside a mouse.

An optical mouse uses light instead of a trackball. A laptop computer uses a touchpad.

A mouse has a **trackball** on the bottom. Inside, there are two rollers that touch the trackball.

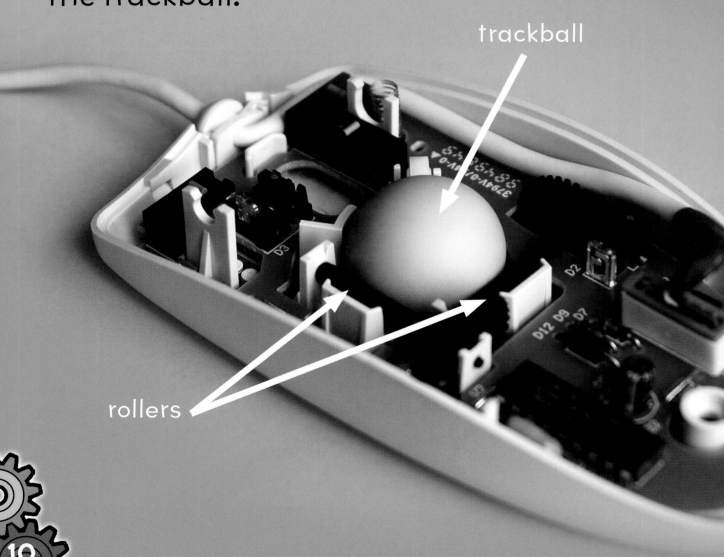

trackball

rollers

Each roller is connected to a wheel.

The wheels have tiny holes in them. **Sensors** near the wheels send and receive light **signals.**

wheels

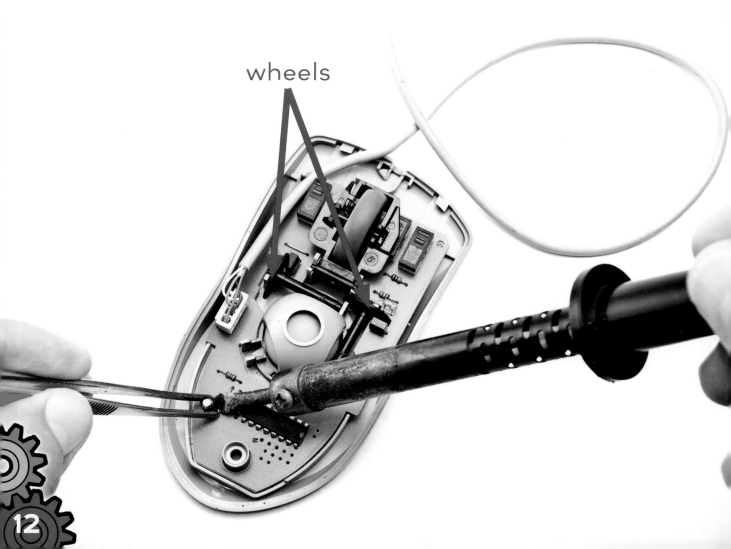

There is also a tiny **computer chip** inside the mouse.

computer chip

Mouse Moves

When you move a mouse, lots of things happen at once. The trackball rolls.

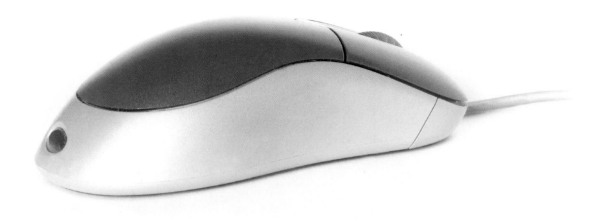

The trackball makes the two rollers spin.

Light shines through the tiny holes.

The light signals go to the sensors. They send information to the computer chip.

The chip sends the information to the computer. It tells the computer how the mouse moved and what buttons were pushed.

Mouse Talk

When you move the mouse, a **cursor** on the computer screen moves too.

Buttons on top of the mouse work like **switches** to talk to the chip inside the mouse.

There are all kinds of computer mice. They all do the same thing: talk to the computer!

Some mice are cordless. They use other ways to send information to the computer.

Photo Glossary

computer chip (kohm-PYOO-ter chip): A small electrical component.

cursor (KUR-sur): A small indicator that shows where you are on a computer screen.

sensors (SEN-surz): Things that can detect changes and send information to another device.

 **signals** (SIG-nuhls): Things that are sent out for communication.

 **switches** (swich-iz): Devices that interrupt the flow in a circuit.

 **trackball** (TRAK-bawl): A pointing device for a computer.

Index

Websites to Visit

www.dougengelbart.org/kids/justforkids.html

computer.howstuffworks.com/mouse2.htm

sloan.stanford.edu/MouseSite

About the Author

Robin Koontz is an author and illustrator of a wide variety of books and articles for children and young adults. Using a mouse makes writing and researching on her computer much easier. She lives with her husband in the Coast Range of western Oregon.

Meet The Author!
www.meetREMauthors.com

www.rourkeeducationalmedia.com

PHOTO CREDITS: Cover, 19, 23 © deepblue4you; title page, page 22 © GlobalStock; page 4 © Sasha burkard; page 5 © MarkRichards; page 6 © LionHector; page 8 © gratvision; page 9 © instagostudio; page 10, 23 © intrdune; page 12 © Alexan24; page 13 © digittalr; page 14 © skynesher; page 15 © karl-kanal; page 16 © Chet Chaimangkhalayon; page 18 © Falko Matte; page 20 © igor terekhov, Petr Malyshev, Alexander Kalina, pete karici, page 21 © karmira; page 23 © Andrei Kovalev

Edited by: Jill Sherman

Cover and Interior design by: Jen Thomas

Library of Congress PCN Data

Computer Mouse/ Robin Koontz
(How It Works)
ISBN (hard cover)(alk. paper) 978-1-62717-641-5
ISBN (soft cover) 978-1-62717-763-4
ISBN (e-Book) 978-1-62717-883-9
Library of Congress Control Number: 2014934208

Printed in the United States of America, North Mankato, Minnesota

Also Available as:

ROURKE'S
e-Books